Beaded Favors

Designs for Needlecases and Treasure Bags

Jennie Might

Published

by

**BLACK
GIRAFFE
DESIGNS**

Beaded Favors is my second book and I'm thrilled to bring you more designs that can be used to create beautiful needlecases and treasure bags. You'll find that *Beaded Favors* contains designs that are a little more detailed than my previous book *Beaded Needlecases*. I hope that you'll enjoy them. Not wanting to exclude the first-time stitcher, I have provided the how-to instruction section from *Beaded Needlecases* in this book. I have increased the number of models to show not only needlecases but treasure bags as well. I hope the gallery will send your imagination soaring! I again use Miyuki Delica beads for my designs and this time have provided the quantities of each color used for the needlecases within each design's key. I hope you will find it useful.

Jennie

ISBN 0-9665853-1-3

Delica® is a registered trademark of Miyuki Shoji Company, Ltd.
Beadscape™ is a trademark of Gigagraphica.
Black Giraffe Designs™ and the Black Giraffe logo are trademarks of Black Giraffe Designs.

Patterns

Materials List

- Miyuki Delica 11º (cylinder or cut)
- #10 or #12 beading needle
- Silamide beading thread in various colors (other beading thread size A or B may be substituted)
- Wooden needlecases 2 1/4" (5.7 cm) high, 1/2" (1.3 cm) diamet
- Accent beads to decorate fringe, neck strap and/or body.
- Scissors or snips to cut thread
- Clear drying glue

Tubular Peyote Instructions

Thread your needle with 60 inches (152 cm) of beading thread. Pick up beads **1** through **36** *(Fig-1)* and tie into a ring with a double knot. Slip this ring of beads onto the bottom of the needlecase. Pick up bead **A** and go through bead **4**. Pick up bead **B** and go through bead **6**. Pick up bead **C** and go through bead **8**. Pick up bead **D** and go through bead **10**. Continue around the needlecase until you come to **R**, the last bead in the row to the right of bead A. Pick up **R**, then go through bead **2**, then **A** and pick up bead **$** and go through bead **B**. Continue until chart is complete. Run your thread through all the beads in the last two rows to strengthen, then bury your thread diagonally down into the beadwork. Snip thread close to the beadwork. Bury the initial tail in the same manner and snip thread close to the beadwork.

Begin lid by stringing the lid first 36 beads and tying into a rin as you did the body. Slip this rin onto the wooden lid that is s attached to the base. Wo upwards until the last row complete. Bury thread after goin diagonally through beadwork secure. Snip thread close beadwork.

Each bead that has a diagor line going through it is the fir bead in each row. The line is the as a guide. The numbers to t right of the charts indicate the ro numbers.

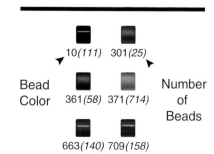

	10(111)	301(25)
Bead Color	361(58) 371(714)	Number of Beads
	663(140)	709(158)

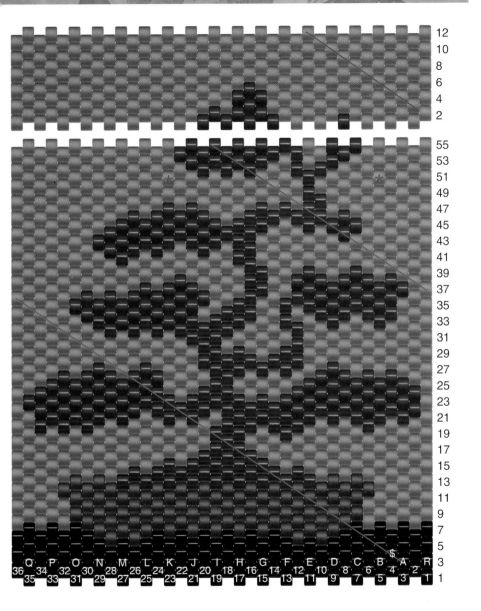

Fig-1 *Even Count Tubular Peyote*

"The true meaning of life is to plant trees,
under whose shade you do not expect to sit."
-Nelson Henderson

To stitch top and bottom, pick up 6 beads and tie into a ring with a square knot. Bring needle through bead 1 and pick up bead 7. Go through bead 2 and pick up bead 8. Follow diagram *(Fig-2)* or **number sequence** to complete. You will stitch two of these, one for the top and one for the bottom of your needlecase.

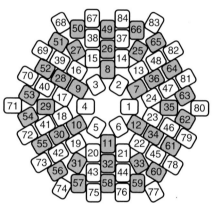

Fig-2 *Flat Circular Peyote*

Once complete, stitch flat circular peyote piece to the lid/base.

Thinly spread a clear dryin glue onto the wood top befo stitching for added security.

The two parts will fit togeth like a zipper. Run needle an thread around again to secur then bury thread diagonally in the beadwork. Snip thread close beadwork. Repeat process attach other flat circular peyo piece.

You are now ready to atta fringe, neck strap, and/ embellishment to your needleca or enjoy as is! Attach neck strap beads with a * in them *(Fig-1)* any beads opposite each other that row.

Hang center fringe by comir out bead 1 and into bead 4 *(Fig-2* Other fringe can hang from bead 7, 8, 9, 10, 11, 12, 25, 27, 29, 31, 3 and 35. Feel free to improvise an hang fringe from any bead yo choose.

Number Sequence

For the Flat Circular Peyote, your needle will go through the bead in the following order: 1, 2, 3, 4, 5, 6, 1, 7, 2, 8, 3, 9, 4, 10, 5, 11, 6, 12, 1, 13, 14, 8, 15, 16, 9, 17, 18, 10, 19, 20, 11, 21, 22, 12, 23, 24, 7, 13, 25, 14, 26 15, 27, 16, 28, 17, 29, 18, 30, 19, 31, 20, 32, 21, 33, 22, 34, 23, 35, 24, 36, 13 25, 37, 26, 38, 27, 39, 28, 40, 29, 41, 30, 42, 31, 43, 32, 44, 33, 45, 34, 46, 35 47, 36, 48, 25, 37, 49, 38, 50, 51, 39, 52, 40, 53, 54, 41, 55, 42, 56, 57, 43, 58 44, 59, 60, 45, 61, 46, 62, 63, 47, 64, 48, 65, 66, 37, 49, 67, 50, 68, 51, 69, 52 70, 53, 71, 54, 72, 55, 73, 56, 74, 57, 75, 58, 76, 59, 77, 60, 78, 61, 79, 62, 80 63, 81, 64, 82, 65, 83, 66, 84.

When you have 6 to 8 inches (15–20 cm) of thread remaining, it is time
attach new thread. Tie a knot in the end of a new length of thread and
p any tail. Remove the old thread from your needle. Thread the new
read into your needle and stitch it into beaded body as shown. Make
re knot disappears into a bead. Exit from the same bead as the old
read. Tie new and old threads together in a square knot at this point.
ntinue your pattern with new thread. Go back and bury the old thread
ter you have added a few more rows. Snip the old thread close to
adwork.

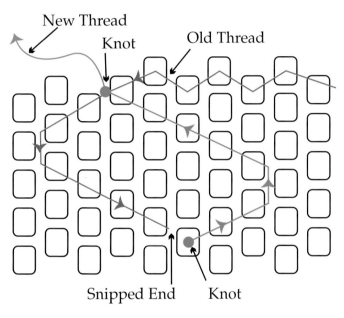

***Fig-3** Starting New Thread*

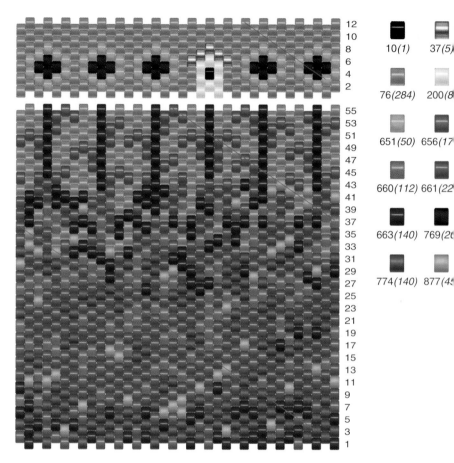

10(1)	37(5)
76(284)	200(8
651(50)	656(17
660(112)	661(22
663(140)	769(2(
774(140)	877(4!

What a lovely favor for a garden lover! Perhaps tuck some seed inside for a gift that will grow!

> No, the heart that has truly lov'd never forgets,
> But as truly loves on to the close,
> As the sun-flower turns on her god, when he sets,
> The same look which she turn'd when he rose.
> -Thomas Moore

It is by believing in roses that one brings them to bloom.
-French proverb

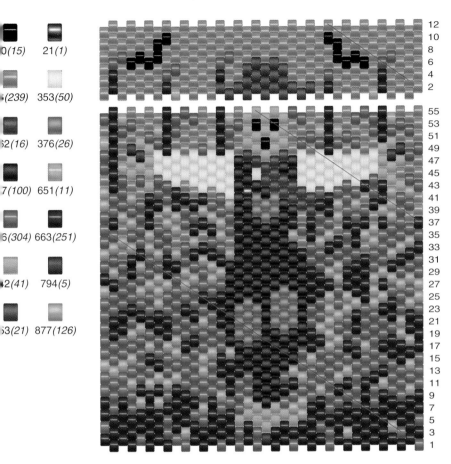

0(15)	21(1)
(239)	353(50)
52(16)	376(26)
7(100)	651(11)
6(304)	663(251)
2(41)	794(5)
53(21)	877(126)

12
10
8
6
4
2

55
53
51
49
47
45
43
41
39
37
35
33
31
29
27
25
23
21
19
17
15
13
11
9
7
5
3
1

air this design with *Home and Garden* and make a wonderful
easure bag. It could contain seeds or a gift certificate for garden
applies.

"A good head and a good heart
are always a formidable combination."
-Nelson Mandela

With time and patience the mulberry leaf becomes a silk gown.
-Chinese proverb

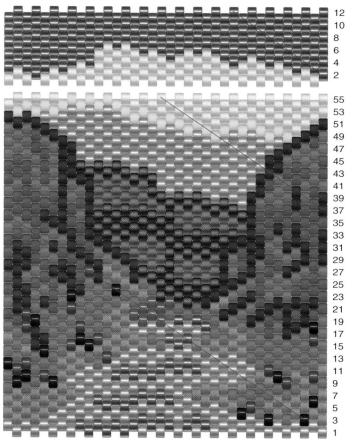

240(219)	243(193)
357(31)	656(16)
663(16)	730(8)
764(120)	777(102)
781(187)	851(112)
852(81)	857(50)
865(71)	

This little bag, I hope, will prove
To be not vainly made;
For should you thread and needles want,
It will afford you aid.

And, as we are about to part,
'T will serve another end;
For, when you look upon this bag,
You'll recollect your friend.
-Jane Austen

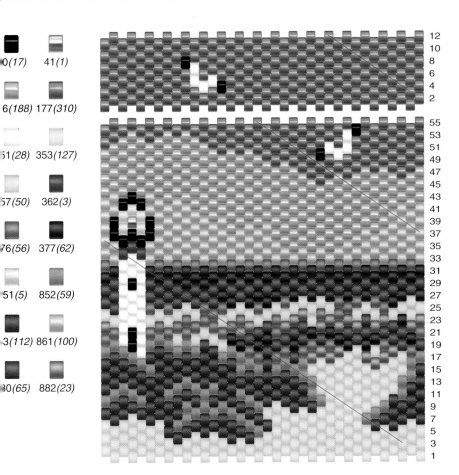

0(17)	41(1)
6(188)	177(310)
51(28)	353(127)
57(50)	362(3)
76(56)	377(62)
51(5)	852(59)
3(112)	861(100)
30(65)	882(23)

What will you hide inside? Some sand from a local or distant shore? Pieces of tumbled glass scented with fragrant oil?

"The voyage of discovery is not in seeking new landscapes
but in having new eyes."
-Marcel Proust

The beautiful is less what one sees than what one dreams.
-Belgian proverb

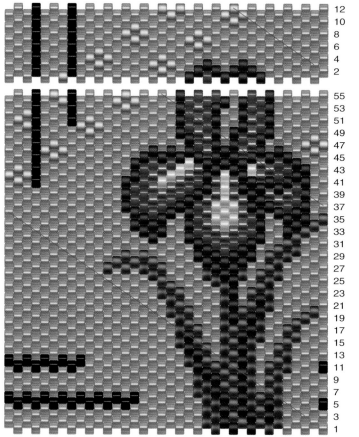

10*(49)*	59*(37)*
80*(9)*	230*(760*
233*(5)*	324*(51)*
327*(31)*	331*(49)*
361*(72)*	373*(58)*
377*(39)*	661*(46)*

"Most of the important things in the world
have been accomplished by people who have kept on trying
when there seemed to be no hope at all."
-Dale Carnegie

Fall seven times, stand up eight.
-Japanese proverb

"He is able who thinks he is able."
-Buddha

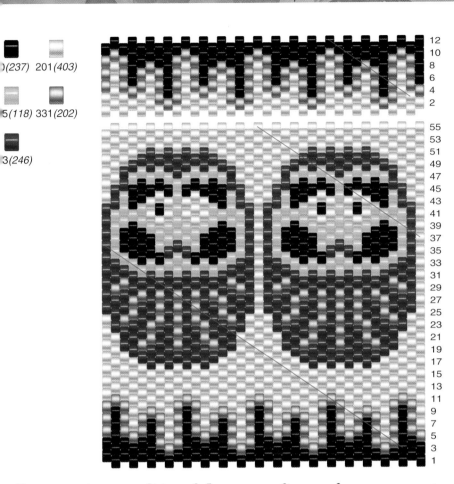

237(237) 201(403)

5(118) 331(202)

3(246)

12
10
8
6
4
2

55
53
51
49
47
45
43
41
39
37
35
33
31
29
27
25
23
21
19
17
15
13
11
9
7
5
3
1

A Daruma is a traditional Japanese figure that represents the pursuit and fulfillment of dreams. Its rotund weighted form keeps it from falling over. The Daruma, like your dreams cannot be kept down. The Daruma comes with blank eyes, and as you fulfill each dream, you give it an eye. It is a solid reminder of what you have accomplished and what you have yet to achieve.

"Go confidently in the direction of your dreams.
Live the life you have imagined."
-Henry David Thoreau

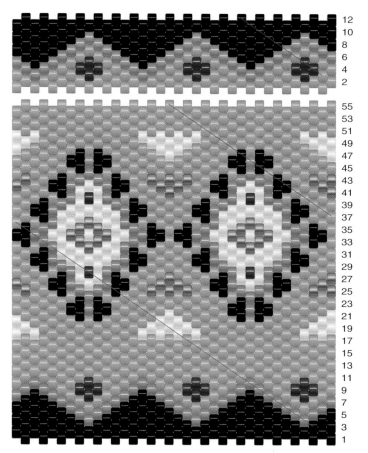

10(282)	200(11(
694(40)	723(28
729(140)	1363(6C

For fans of the American Southwest, here is a design based upo Navajo blankets. What will you roll up in your blanket?

May the Warm Winds of Heaven blow softly upon your house.
May the Great Spirit bless all who enter there.
May your Moccasins make happy tracks in many snows,
and may the Rainbow always touch your shoulder.
-Cherokee Prayer Blessing

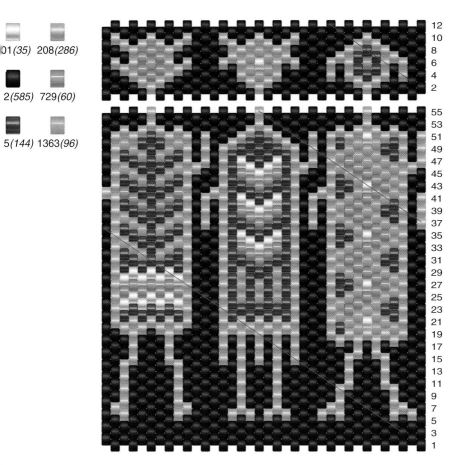

01(35)   208(286)

2(585)   729(60)

5(144)   1363(96)

Go ahead, swap their heads! They won't mind. These three
shamen will be happy to carry a prayer for you. Maybe bits of
turquoise for protection or some amber for healing?

"Great spirits have always encountered
violent opposition from mediocre minds."
-Albert Einstein

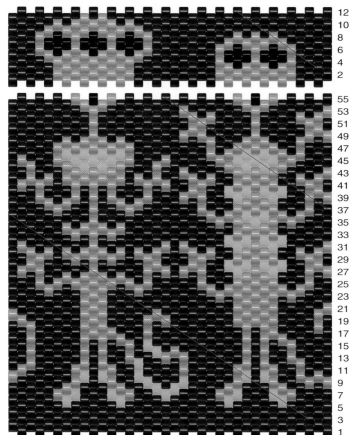

10(22)	278(755
733(371)	763(58)

Our friendly aliens Greech and Glift have so many hands and s little to do. Can they be your messengers? Bearing "get well wishes? Or a "hello" note from across the miles? They'd b happy to perform any task.

"Somewhere, something incredible
is waiting to be known."
-Carl Sagan

"The most beautiful thing we can experience
is the mysterious."
-Albert Einstein

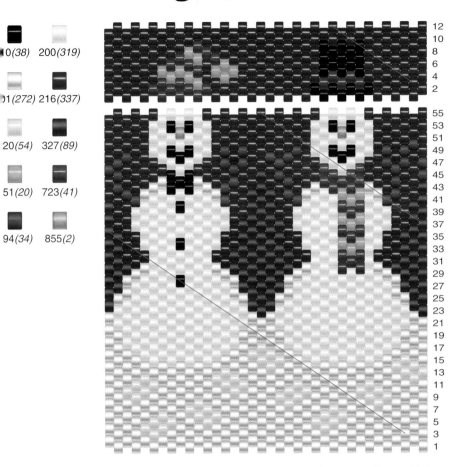

0(38)	200(319)
1(272)	216(337)
20(54)	327(89)
51(20)	723(41)
94(34)	855(2)

rosty snowmen Up and Down are ready for anything! You can nix or match their hats to the rest of their attire. Tiny mints vould stay icy cool with these guys keeping their frigid watch.

"A sense of humor is like a needle and thread;
it will patch up so many things."
-Unknown

"When you are content to be simply yourself and don't compare or compete, everybody will respect you."
-Lao-tzu

12
10
8   203(72) 277(868)
6
4
2   331(266)

55
53
51
49
47
45
43
41
39
37
35
33
31
29
27
25
23
21
19
17
15
13
11
9
7
5
3
1

The Star of David and the Chai. Chai is the Hebrew symbol for life. Perhaps this favor will bring you or someone you love good luck!

"Your cheeks are comely with rows of jewels,
your neck with strings of beads."
-Song of Songs, 1:10

"... for my heart rejoiced in all my labor,
and this was my portion of all my labor."
-Ecclesiastes, 2:10

(699)	31(304)
45(7)	211(196)

This 7-branched menorah is loosely patterned after the menorah in the Holy Temple. It is not a menorah for Chanukah. A Chanukah menorah would consist of 9 branches, the middle branch being higher than the others.

"You have ravished my heart, my sister, my bride,
you have ravished my heart with one of your eyes,
with one link of your necklace."
-Song of Songs, 4:9

A very special thank you to Sandra Lynne Stern and Esther Liberman for their guidance and suggestions for these two pages.

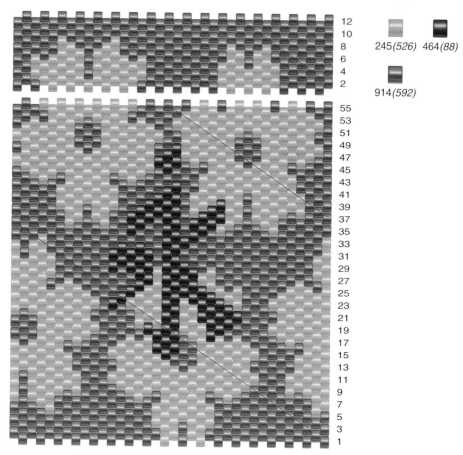

12
10
8
6
4
2

245*(526)*   464*(88)*

914*(592)*

55
53
51
49
47
45
43
41
39
37
35
33
31
29
27
25
23
21
19
17
15
13
11
9
7
5
3
1

This Japanese character upon the cherry blossoms is the Kanji ideogram for "Forever".

"Destiny is not a matter of chance,
it is a matter of choice;
it is not a thing to be waited for,
it is a thing to be achieved."
-William Jennings Bryan

45(514) 464(107)

14(585)

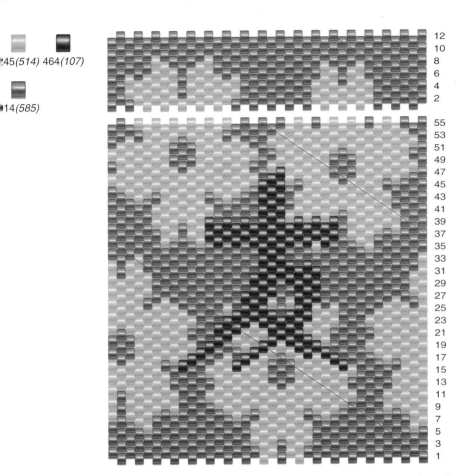

This Japanese character upon the cherry blossoms is the Kanji ideogram for "Friend". A special gift for a special friend? Use both designs to make a sentimental treasure bag.

"When I find myself fading,
I close my eyes and realize
my friends are my energy."
-Anonymous

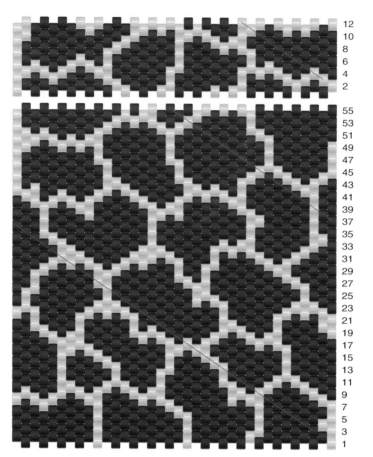

732(336) 764(870)

I couldn't help including some wild animal print designs. It could add a bit of the savannah into your sewing kit or wardrobe.

"Your bounty is beyond my speaking,
But though my mouth be dumb,
My heart shall thank you."
-Nicholas Rowe

"It is most true, stylus virum arguit,- our style betrays us."
-Robert Burton

0(725) 211(481)

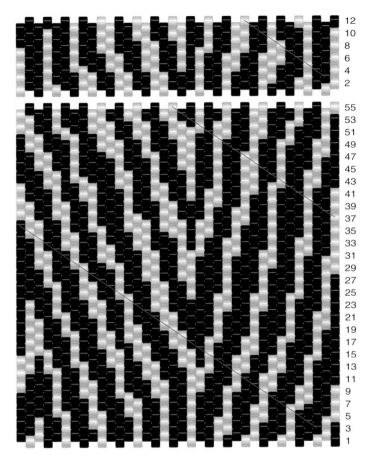

Take a stroll down to the water hole and mingle with the wildlife. What can you put into this exotic favor? Maybe, a ticket to the zoo?

God, grant me the Serenity to accept the things I cannot change,
Courage to change the things I can,
And Wisdom to know the difference
-The Serenity Prayer

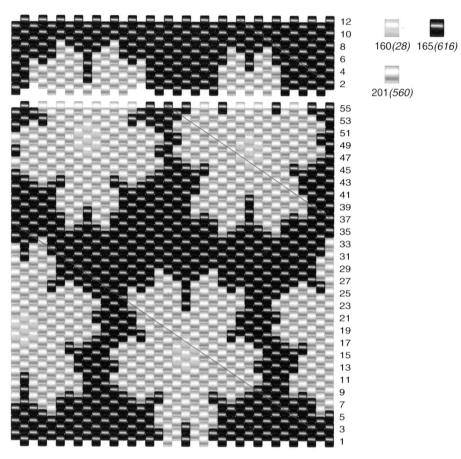

160 *(28)*	165 *(616)*
201 *(560)*	

This design shows you what a little color change can do! This is the same background as the *Friend* and *Forever in Bloom* patterns but using different colors. The flowers are now lemon blossoms.

"You, yourself,
as much as anybody
in the entire universe,
deserve your love and affection."
-Buddha

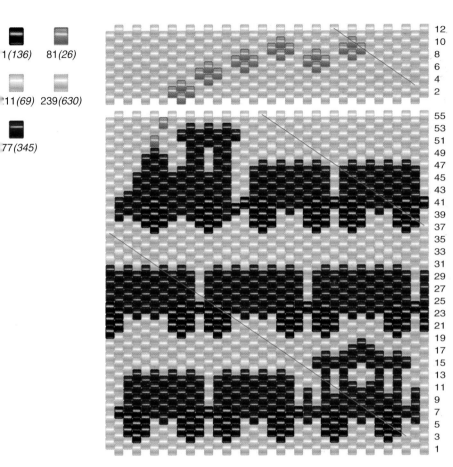

1 *(136)*   81 *(26)*

11 *(69)*   239 *(630)*

77 *(345)*

12
10
8
6
4
2

55
53
51
49
47
45
43
41
39
37
35
33
31
29
27
25
23
21
19
17
15
13
11
9
7
5
3
1

From the Land of Lost Teeth comes the Tooth Train. It is kept ever so busy with all the children and hockey players in the world! You don't really think that the Tooth Fairy collects all those teeth by herself do you? And what about all that heavy coinage she leaves behind?? The Tooth Train rides the rails of Zzzzzzz and helps keep the Tooth Fairy on track.

"For where your treasure is,
there will your heart be also."
-Matthew 6:21

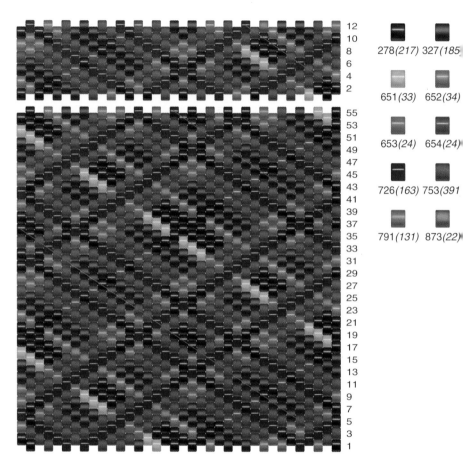

278(217)	327(185)
651(33)	652(34)
653(24)	654(24)
726(163)	753(391)
791(131)	873(22)

For the Scotsman or Scotswoman you love. Perhaps tuck in their clan's motto? To my knowledge, this is not the tartan for any particular clan. I loosely started from our familial MacDonald tartan, then added more colors and lines for visual interest.

"Gaol, Dilseachd, Cairdeas"
-ancient Gaelic words for "Love, Loyalty, Friendship"

Wink at small faults, for you have great ones yourself.
-Scottish proverb

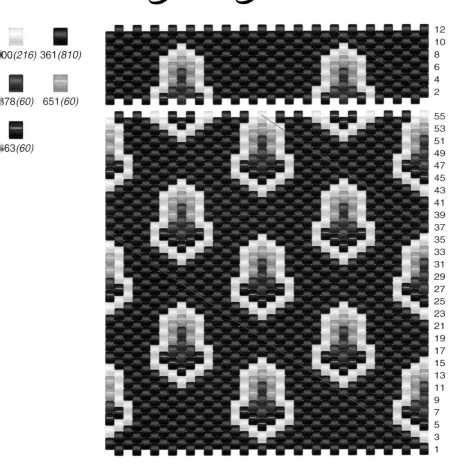

00(216) 361(810)

378(60) 651(60)

63(60)

nspired by French hand blocked fabrics from the region of Provence. All four color ways are charming and traditional.

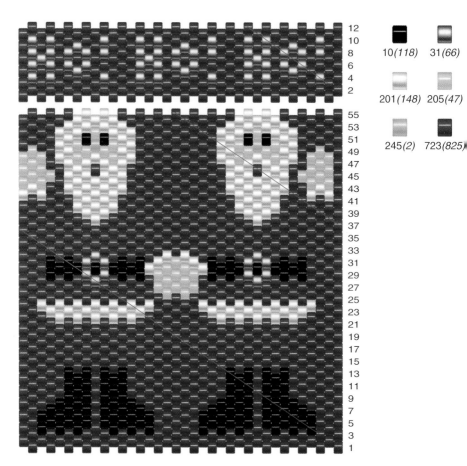

Let our merry Santas be the bearers of jolly tidings for you. I
you've been good - some new needles perhaps? If you've been
naughty - some broken and uneven beads?

"When you share your joy with others,
You double each smile and each laugh.
When you share your pain and sorrow,
Each tear is divided in half."
-Unknown

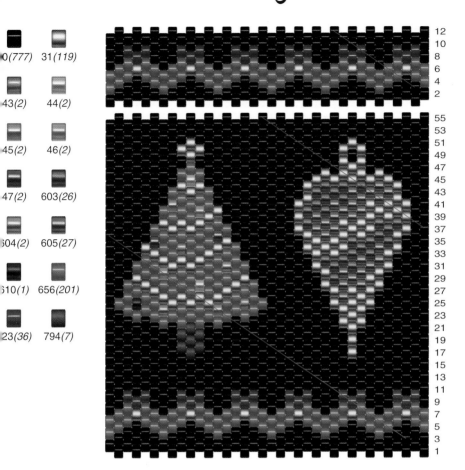

0(777)   31(119)

43(2)   44(2)

45(2)   46(2)

47(2)   603(26)

604(2)   605(27)

610(1)   656(201)

23(36)   794(7)

A decorated tree, an ornament and garlands with bows all round. A festive design to help ring in the Christmas season!

Fear less, hope more;
Whine less, breathe more;
Talk less, say more;
hate less, love more;
And all good things are yours.
-Swedish proverb

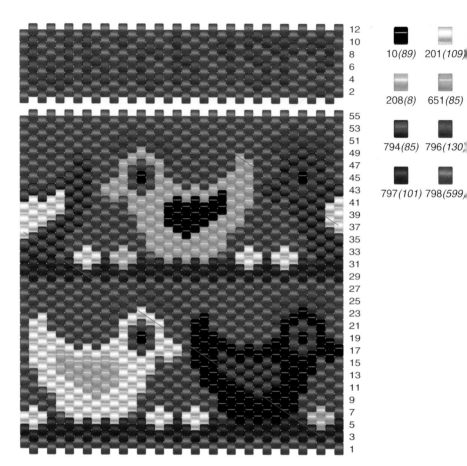

10 *(89)* 201 *(109)*

208 *(8)* 651 *(85)*

794 *(85)* 796 *(130)*

797 *(101)* 798 *(599)*

Which came first, the chicken or the egg? You won't find the answer here! You may however find yourself putting some other equally age old mystifying question into this lively favor.

"Noise proves nothing.
Often a hen who has merely laid an egg
cackles as if she had laid an asteroid."
-Mark Twain

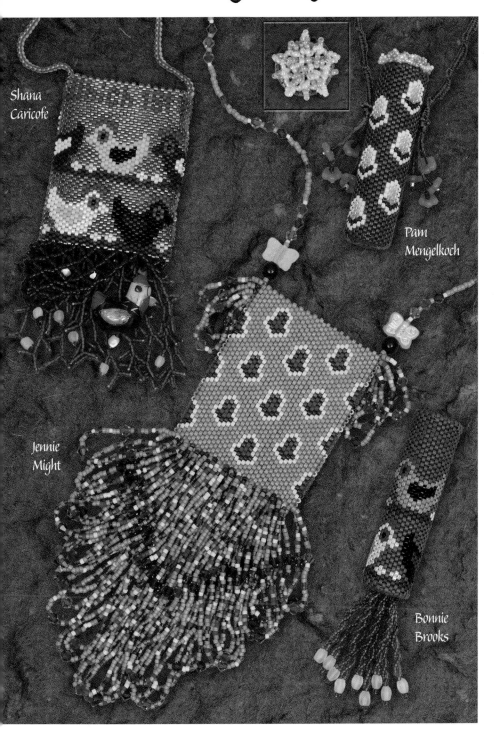

Shana Caricofe

Pam Mengelkoch

Jennie Might

Bonnie Brooks

Debbie
Williams

Debbie
Williams

Pam
Mengelkoch

Pam
Mengelkoch

Shana
Caricote

Debbie
Williams

Caroline
Bleil

Debbie
Williams

Lampwork by
Karen Jordon

Debbie
Williams

Jennie
Might

Debbie Williams
& Jennie Might

Suzanne
Cooper

Kathy
Rice

Trudy
Merchant

Shana
Caricofe

Debbie
Williams

Debbie
Williams

Lampwork by
Cheryl Lynn
Keggan
of Dragon Beads

Esther
Liberman

Jennie
Might

Esther
Liberman

Jennie
Might

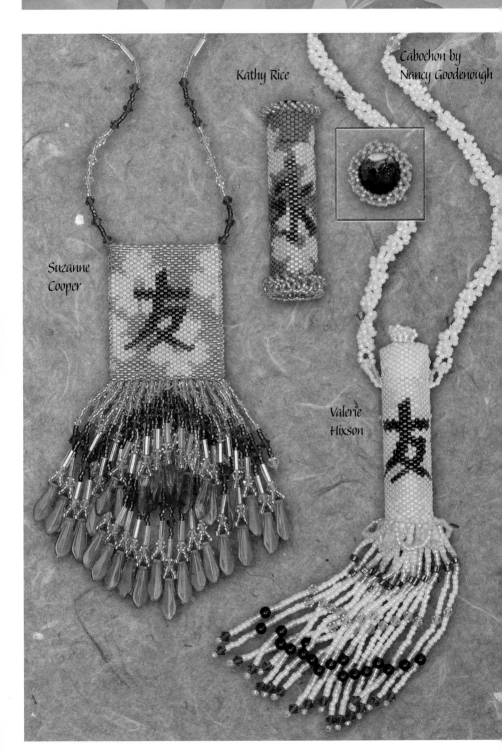

Kathy Rice

Cabochon by
Nancy Goodenough

Suzanne
Cooper

Valerie
Hixson

Katie Magill

Debbie
Williams

Bonnie Brooks

Debbie Williams

Pam Mengelkoch

Shana Caricofe

Debbie Williams

Cisco
Cosgrove

Cisco
Cosgrove

Caroline
Bleil

Debbie Williams

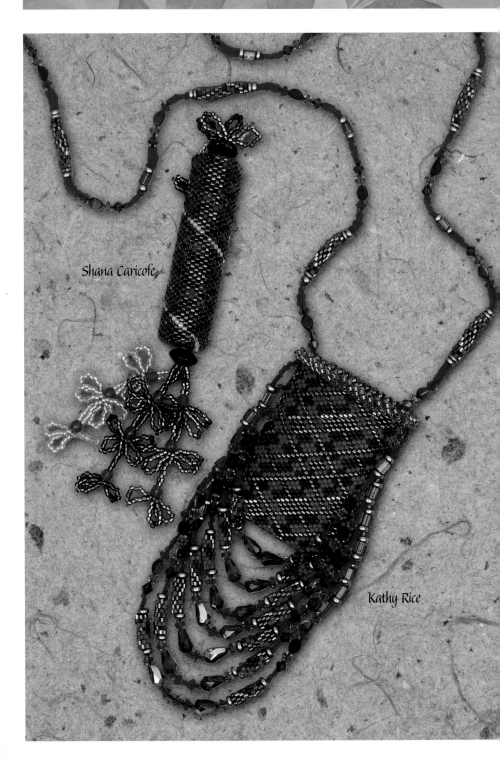

Shana Caricofe

Kathy Rice

There are so many items you can tuck away within your beaded favor. You may desire to print out one of the quotes or poems within this book or write a poem of your own. Here are few filler suggestions to help you on your way.

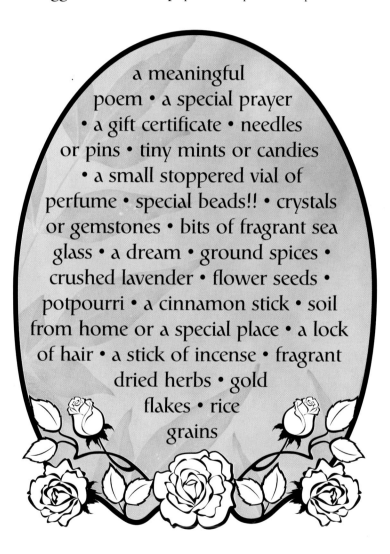

a meaningful
poem • a special prayer
• a gift certificate • needles
or pins • tiny mints or candies
• a small stoppered vial of
perfume • special beads!! • crystals
or gemstones • bits of fragrant sea
glass • a dream • ground spices •
crushed lavender • flower seeds •
potpourri • a cinnamon stick • soil
from home or a special place • a lock
of hair • a stick of incense • fragrant
dried herbs • gold
flakes • rice
grains

The following are birthflowers and birthstones attributed to each month to help you choose the correct seeds or stones to place inside your beaded favor for a thoughtful birthday gift.

Month	Flower	Stone
January	Carnation	Garnet
February	Violet	Amethyst
March	Jonquil	Aquamarine
April	Sweet Pea	Diamond
May	Lily of the Valley	Emerald
June	Rose	Pearl
July	Larkspur, Delphinium	Ruby
August	Gladiolus	Peridot; Onyx
September	Aster	Sapphire
October	Marigold	Opal
November	Chrysanthemum	Topaz; Citrine
December	Narcissus	Turquoise; Zircon

Here are some meanings for a few herbs and spices to deliver fragrant added message when hidden within your beaded favor.

Cinnamon - Energy in adversity

Cloves - Lasting friendship, Dignity

Basil - Romance

Bay - Protection

Catnip - Courage

Oregano - Banishes Sadness

Chamomile - Energy

Parsley - Festivity, Rejoicing

Rosemary - Remembrance, Protection from illness

Marjoram - Joy, Happiness

Sage - Wisdom, Esteem, Alleviation of Grief

Thyme - Strength, Courage, Bravery

Mint - Virtue, Wisdom

Nutmeg - Increase mental acuity

Lavender - Silence

Cumin - Fidelity

Blank Graph

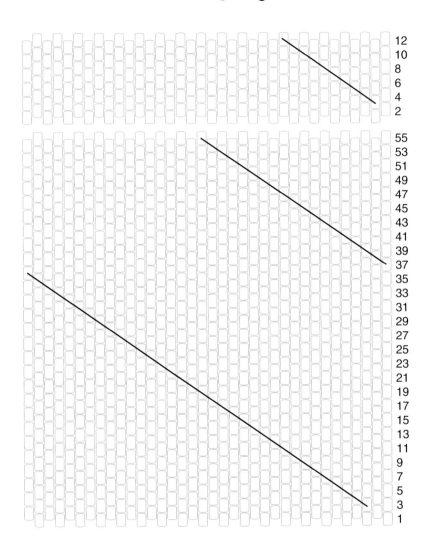

Copy this page and design your own beaded favor.

Designs in this book were created using Beadscape™2.0 "Beadwork Design Software for Macintosh" by Gigagraphica. For more information write to:

Gigagraphica
958 Vetch Circle
Lafayette, CO 80026

http://www.gigagraphica.com/beadscape
email: gigagraphica@earthlink.net

If wooden needlecases are unavailable in your area, you can contact:

Black Giraffe Designs
P.O.Box 934,
Round Rock, TX 78680-0934

Inquires can also be directed to:

http://www.blackgiraffe.com
email: needlecase@blackgiraffe.com